Introducing Rabbits

Everyone is aware of rabbits for they are such cute little animals, especially when they are young. What many people do not always realize is just how many different varieties there are these days, and the fact that they are not rodents, as is often thought. Further, you might be surprised to find that they are not just children's pets but enjoy a vast following from dedicated adult fanciers who breed and exhibit them for their many coat colors, patterns and textures.

Rabbits are members of the zoological order of animals known as Lagomorpha. Their nearest relatives are hares, there being about 44 species of these two animals, 25 of which are rabbits. They are all grouped in the family called Leporidae.

Hares have longer hind legs and ears than do rabbits. They

This is a Russian-bred Chinchilla rabbit. It is a breed from which inexpensive fur coats are made.

This is a New Zealand rabbit. It comes in three color varieties: black, red, and white.

This is a female Belgian Hare. ➤

spend most of their time above ground and nest in hollows, whereas rabbits prefer to live in warrens. These burrows may extend long distances under the ground to form complex networks with numerous entrances. Rabbits are found in most countries but are not native to the Antarctic and are an introduced species to Australia. The rabbits kept as pets all over the world are descendants of the species which was native to Spain and North Africa. It has the scientific name of *Oryctolagus cuniculus*. From this the many domesticated breeds have been developed over the centuries, probably from about the early 16th century onwards when monks in Europe bred them as a food and fur source. Prior to this rabbits were kept from the days of the Romans, but these were retained in

A mixed-breed rabbit. Rabbits are popular not only as pets but also as a source of fur and meat. ➤

◀ Closeup of the head of a Belgian Hare.

enclosures or *Lepororii* —walled gardens originally built to keep hares enclosed. There were no attempts to selectively breed them, so any mutations which may have appeared passed unnoticed or were regarded as freaks not worth keeping.

Today, there are hundreds of breeds found around the world but many of these are seen only in their country of development. In the USA, Canada and Great Britain you have a wide choice ranging from the very well known to those which are rare. Yet others are relatively new breeds still being developed in the age old manner of hybridization and the transfer of

A white, short-haired Rex, red-eyed albino. This breed has plush, velvet-like fur.

gene mutations from one breed to another.

Rabbits are extremely easy pets to care for, so easy in fact that millions of them are subjected to a very miserable existence in housing that is totally unsuited to them. They are fed on poor diets, and the result is a very sad animal. Such rabbits are not seen at their best because they are very social creatures that need the company of their own kind. They tame easily and make delightful pets if only you will give them the attention they deserve - this will be amply rewarded in the pleasure they can provide, either as pets or as breeding and exhibition stock.

This little book covers all of the most important aspects of rabbit management and concludes by discussing a number of breeds, some popular and some less so - but all excellent possibilities for the first-time owner.

Rabbits that have long fur will need regular grooming to look their best.

There are several breeds of Chinchilla rabbit. All have the same coloration, but they vary in size.

3

A pair of *New Zealand Whites*. These are pink-eyed albinos. ☞

Choosing a Rabbit

If you are obtaining your first pet rabbit, or one for your children, then I would strongly recommend that you consider the following points very carefully.

1. Avoid purchasing any breed that has been physically altered during its development and which, as a result, may involve you in extra work. For example, the Lop breed has very long ears which can be the source of problems if you do not ensure the rabbit is kept in spotless conditions. The Angora is a gorgeous breed but its coat requires a lot of attention if it is not to become a bedraggled mess. Miniature breeds may experience incorrect tooth alignment or other genetic problems.

These breeds are best obtained once you are sure you really do have the time and interest in maintaining them - and have gained practical experience in keeping rabbits.

☜ A *Netherland Dwarf* female.

2. It is always better to have two rabbits than one - they will keep each other company. Start with two does unless you plan to breed. Two bucks may well start fighting each other once they mature - and certainly will if they sense a female in the area. Even females may become aggressive to their hutch companion, but usually they are fine if brought up together and are living in spacious accommodation. Alternatively, you might find that one or more guinea pigs will make ideal companions for rabbits. Both get along real well with each other.

A *Netherland Dwarf* male. ☞

3. Commence with purebred rabbits. They cost no more to keep than crossbreeds. Pet quality

An albino *longhaired rabbit.*

examples are modest in price when compared with other pets such as cats or dogs.

4. If you plan to breed or exhibit your pet you are strongly advised to seek out high quality stock - this will prove the better investment in the long run and less expensive than trying to upgrade via a breeding program. You should also obtain stock that is mature enough for its quality to be seen, yet young enough to have a good breeding or exhibition life. Very young rabbits are therefore not the best choice - you will enjoy the pleasure of these as you breed with your foundation stock.

5. If the rabbit is to be a child's pet you should be prepared to take over all of the daily chores if the child fails to attend to these. Many children lose interest in their pets after the initial enthusiasm for them starts to wane and the pets grow up. If you are at all unsure on this account then it is better not to let the child have the rabbit.

Where to Purchase

Most pet shops that sell livestock will have rabbits for sale. These will be pet quality and ideal for a beginner's purposes.

This lop rabbit is called a *German Ram* in Europe.

The English Spot rabbit is a pet breed.

If you later decide to get involved with exhibition-class animals, your dealer can obtain stock for you or steer you to a source.

Age to Purchase

Rabbits are normally fully independent of their mother by the age of 5-8 weeks, depending on the breed, so any time after this is fine for you to take them home. The owner should assure you that the youngsters are eating well and have been weaned from their mother if they are clearly very young.

◆ This is a black *Polish* rabbit. It is one of the many colors and breeds available from your pet shop. Rabbits (bunnies) are mostly sold around Easter.

If you are thinking about buying an Easter bunny as a gift for someone else's child, talk to their parents first. Rabbits are wonderful, undemanding pets, but they do need regular daily attention. ◗

◆ A good rabbit hutch will be draft-free and well ventilated.

The Healthy Youngster

Your first guide to the likely health of a rabbit will be in the accommodation it is living in. This must be very clean and indicate that the owner gives hygiene a high priority. The food and water vessels should be clean and there should be no undue smell from the hutches or rabbitry.

Baby rabbits are adorable and should be lively. Their fur will be smooth and their skin will exhibit no signs of bald patches or abrasions. It is most important that their eyes are round and clear, with no indications of weeping. The same is true of the nose, which should display no discharge whatsoever. Such symptoms might indicate the early stages of myxomatosis, or 'snuffles', a deadly disease which is one of the many conditions related to potentially lethal bacterial diseases. In the latter case the front paws will often be wet and stained from the rabbit wiping its face consistently. The vent area of a healthy rabbit will not appear stained from liquid fecal matter. The teeth should be inspected to see that they are neatly aligned - the upper incisors just overlapping those of the lower jaw. A condition called malocclusion is created by poorly aligned teeth. This can result in the teeth growing to such an extent that the rabbit cannot feed - it is not unheard of for the teeth to actually grow through a jaw! Overgrown teeth can be trimmed by your vet, but such rabbits should never be bred from (nor purchased if the condition is seen) as it has a genetic base, so may be passed on to future generations.

Look inside the rabbit's ears to check these are clean and fresh smelling. Rabbits, especially if they have large or drooping ears, are rather prone to ear mites. These produce brown flaky canker-like growths that can be a real nuisance once established. It is wise to check a few of the youngsters, both to satisfy yourself as to the one you want and also to see that none are in any way affected by the conditions described. If one is,

← The *Polish* bunny is a very small breed of rabbit. Its ideal weight is 2 $1/2$ pounds.

→ This trio of Netherland Dwarfs is about to be transported to a rabbit show.

◊ Daddy on the left and Mommy on the right with their two *kids* in between. Pure bred rabbits produce predictable offspring. It costs just as much to raise inferior rabbits as it does to raise pure bred rabbits. Invest wisely initially and get good quality rabbits.

← This type of cage is suitable for transporting pet rabbits, but it is way too small to serve as permanent housing.

↓ An ideal outdoor hutch for your pet rabbit. It is easy to care for and perfect for keeping and breeding rabbits.

Pet shops which only sell bunnies for Easter use temporary cages for their stock like this one. These are KD (Knock-Down) cages which come apart for easy storage. Perhaps your local pet supplier can get one for you? ➤

there is a good chance the rest of the litter may be carrying the problem, even if it has not advanced to the visible stage at that moment.

If you are planning to purchase a show or breeding rabbit then you must either take a person knowledgeable in that breed with you or - which is your better option in practical terms - to rely on the integrity of the seller.

Accommodations

The needs of rabbits in respect to their housing are very simple. However, a great many are forced to live in very unsuitable homes because their owners have given very little thought to the matter, working on the premise that a hutch is a hutch. Nothing could be further from the truth. Seeing rabbits cooped up in tiny hutches to live out their lives after their owners have lost interest in them is always very sad - so make every effort to provide a roomy, draft free and well ventilated hutch from the very outset. Better still, why not provide them with their own little enclosure so that when you are away during the day they too can enjoy some fresh air and generally move around and exercise. They will look better and feel better.

An *English Spot* female. These rabbits have lovely markings and coloring.

The Basic Hutch

The hutch you choose can be as elaborate as you care to make it, but it should be suited to its function. An indoor hutch, or one well protected from inclement weather, can be of lighter construction than one which must withstand all weathers. Even so, it should still

A *Satin Angora* raised for its fur. Angora fur is used in the manufacture of various kinds of clothing.

A Russian breed known as the *Soviet Marder*.

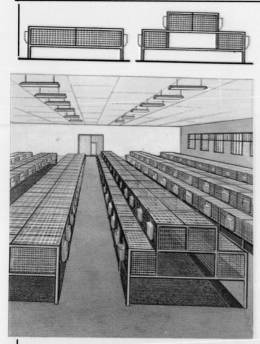

be reasonably substantial so it will give you years of good service. You can purchase hutches from some pet shops but these are rarely designed for outdoor or lengthy service. Further, the cost factors are such that they are usually of inadequate size: they are designed for low cost sale rather than with consideration for the rabbits. They make fine temporary housing but you will obtain a much better hutch if you design and make it yourself suited to your needs.

You can purchase commercial breeding units which are designed for the person with many rabbits. Here we are concerned with the pet owner, or the keeper who wishes to breed on a very small scale.

Size: For a single rabbit of average size you should think in terms of about 93cm long, 45cm deep and 45cm high (36x18x18in). This is larger than some might suggest but I regard this as the very minimum. If it is to house two pets then a slightly larger unit can be designed. The larger and more comfortable the hutch, the less likely your pets are to gnaw at it. Materials: Use exterior plywood with a minimum of 1.25cm (1/2in) thickness. This can be mounted on a frame of timber 5x5cm (2x2in). If you really want to insulate it well you could add a lining wall and fill the space with polystyrene or similar material. The lining (inner) wall could be of a thinner board. It is always better to cover the roof with materials that will make it really waterproof.

▲ This is a set-up for an indoor rabbitry where rabbits are raised on a commercial basis. Two types of cages are used. The double cages are back-to-back. The triple cages are one atop the other as shown in the sketches above.

◄ Outdoor hutches are necessary for breeds raised for their fur. They need the cold weather to develop a thick coat of fur. The arrow indicates that the foundation should go far below the frost line. The hutch bottom is screened so the droppings fall onto the ground, where earthworms thrive on them.

In order to protect the inner walls of the hutch from urine, you can cover these to half their height with clear plastic sheeting. This can be screwed (not stuck) on so that it can be removed easily for cleaning or replacement. A removable aluminum metal tray is a feature of many hutches. This protects the floor from absorbing urine. You could again use plastic sheeting. I prefer neither as my hutches have a toilet room. This has a plastic base screwed into position. All areas are given numerous coats of paint and have a good base of sawdust and shavings. With regular cleaning (at least once a week) the hutches remain in really good shape and free from urine stains. I should add that my rabbits also have free access to an enclosure, so much of their toiletry needs are done in this, which greatly aids in keeping the hutch clean. Rabbits are very clean animals so a hutch only smells foul if its owner allows it to by neglect and by poor design of the unit.

You will need some weldwire mesh to place on the front of the living area. This can be uncoated (galvanized) or plastic coated, the latter looking nicer and giving even longer life. The hole size should be small enough to prevent mice or rats (or snakes if they are common in your area) from entering the hutch, 2.5x 2.5cm (1x1in) is usually adequate. You will need latches and hinges for doors depending on the design.

Dutch rabbits are genetically pure and breed true to form and color. ▲

▲ This rabbit has a white collar and white boots. It is a dwarf rabbit.

▲ Dwarf silvers are a seemingly rare breed only because they are not popular. Intensive inbreeding could easily fix the color of these rabbits.

This home-made hutch is very ample for raising a family of rabbits. ◀

A home-made hutch for colony keeping and breeding. The hutch is kept off the ground so no predators (like dogs) can have easy access to the trapped rabbits. The wood can be any outdoor kind of lumber. ▶

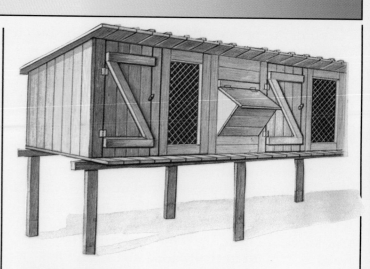

▼ The smaller the rabbit, like this dwarf, the more animals can be kept in the hutch shown above right. It is best to have only one male in any group of rabbits.

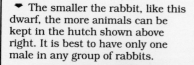

▼ The inside of a very practical hutch. The floor boards are removable so that they can be inverted from time to time, and they can easily be cleaned.

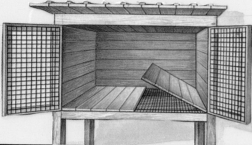

Design Features

Essentially, a practical hutch is a rectangular box in which there are two or three compartments. It will be raised on legs so that there is at least 15cm (6in) of clear space beneath the hutch to allow for plenty of floor ventilation (and so mice cannot use this as a refuge). It will have a sloping roof so rainwater will drain from the back end. The roof should overhang the walls to provide some protection to these from all weathers, including sunshine. Inside, there should be a small sleeping area, and a large living area, a corner of which will be used as a toilet. You may include a separate toilet compartment and this will be used as such if provided. Access from the 'bedroom' to the living area is via a small hole placed towards the back of the hutch - the hole should be just large enough for the rabbit to go through. This room will have a door to the front of the hutch so you can easily clean it out. The mesh for the living area is best placed on a frame and this can be hinged to open either down or sideways. Ours are not

Inside a commercial rabbitry in Russia. The rabbits shown in these cages are being offered for sale by lots. You buy the cageful or none!

A very alert Netherland Dwarf. It is a male. ➡

➡ This is a home-made hutch. The upper part is for the pair to mate and have their young. The lower part is for the offspring. The bottom of the cages is screening. The tray between the cages enables the droppings to fall to the ground, where the earthworms thrive on them. A side-line for many rabbit growers is the sale of earthworms.

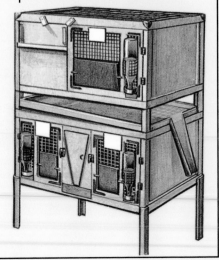

hinged but free units that can be taken out totally when the living area is cleaned. They are held in place by swivel latches and the frame to the mesh fits flush with the front of the hutch - small wood struts inside the hutch keep it in place. If a toilet area is fitted this is placed next to the living area and entered by a small opening - again with a door to the outside. You may fit a sliding or other door to the sleeping area so that you can clean the living quarters whilst retaining the rabbits in their den. If you wish to allow your pets free access to an enclosure this can be provided via a sliding door placed next to the toilet compartment. From this a ramp with wooden struts across it allows them to clamber down to floor level. The sliding door enables you to keep them in the hutch if required. The hutch should be placed onto suitable slabs or a concrete base so that the shavings, feces, etc. are easy to sweep up.

The exterior walls of the hutch should be well protected either by wood preservatives or by generous coats of paint. The inner walls should be painted with a non lead washable paint - and one which has been treated with an acaracide chemical is even better and will give some protection against mites, lice and similar unwanted creatures.

 Lops are rabbits with drooping ears. They come in many colors. Special colors and breeds can be ordered from your local pet supplier. There is a wonderful book by Sandy Crook entitled *LOP RABBITS AS PETS*, P.S.-809; ISBN 0-86622-137-9.

This is a commercial set up. The numbers are comparative. For example, **400** can be 20 feet, so each measurement can be exactly calculated by using fractions. In addition to the rooms that house rabbits, there is also an examination room, a hospital room, and a utility room. ➧

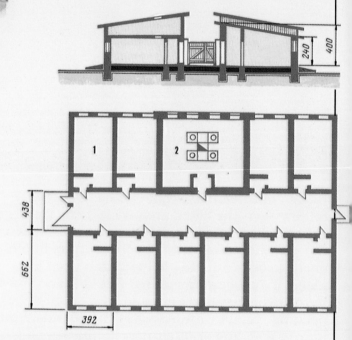

The Hutch Site

The best site for a hutch is in a sheltered position, but one which has the viewing mesh facing south so it enjoys the benefit of the morning sunshine. However, it should be placed so that there is always some shadow within the hutch in order that the rabbit can retreat from

⬧Unless you are breeding for fur or meat, the best rabbits to breed are dwarfs. They are available in many colors and require half the space of meat rabbits. There is a great book on dwarf rabbits called *DWARF RABBITS* by Günther Flauaus. H-1073, ISBN 0-86622-671-0. All TFH books are available at your local pet shop.

direct sunshine without having to retire to its sleeping quarters. During very bad weather it is useful if you have a sheet of clear plastic that can be quickly hooked and secured to the front mesh. This can be a little shorter than the full height so it allows plenty of air in - the opening will be protected by the roof overhang. Try to avoid sites where the hutch front is open to driving winds and rain - remember, wild rabbits are normally real snug in their deep burrows and quickly suffer if exposed to damp and drafty conditions.

Your pet rabbit should have an enclosure so it can run around and get some exercise. Keeping a rabbit penned in a small cage will not kill it, but the rabbit will become muscle bound. ◄

Enclosures

Ideally, your pet should have access to an enclosure so it can run around and exercise. This can either be an open enclosure surrounded by a wall or suitable weldmesh fence, or it can be a covered one that allows the rabbit freedom even when you are away from home. You could build a portable unit that can be placed on different sections of your garden by rotation. In this way the bunny can have a fresh supply of grass

◄ Don't expect your rabbit to differentiate between its food and its cage lining. Unless their food is kept isolated, the rabbits will dirty it with their waste matter.

Rabbits of different breeds and sizes should be kept separately. Large rabbits could injure dwarfs.
◄

Art. # H-291

Art. # H-293

Art. # H-301

Art. # H-307

without ever overgrazing it.

The hutch described in this chapter is of a design that you will normally have to build yourself. It will cost much more than the value of the rabbits it will probably house. However, it really is worth investing in good accommodation. You can make the design simpler but do try to ensure that its size is generous and that the materials used are of a substantial nature. Designing your rabbit's home can be fun for all the family and will certainly make for much better enjoyment of your pets.

◀ Your local pet supplier has a whole line of Hagen travel cages for rabbits.

◀ Carry cages for rabbits are necessary if you want to take your rabbit anyplace.

Bedding and Living Area Coverings

There are numerous potential materials for covering the floors. 1. **Sawdust** (choose the lighter-colored types) is traditional and absorbs urine very well. Be sure it is from wood not treated with harmful chemicals. 2. **Granulated paper** is an alternative to sawdust and is clearly less dusty. Shredded paper makes a cosy bedding material.

3 **Hay.** This is the preferred choice for the bedding compartment as it is very snug and, of course, an excellent food. Be sure it is dry and as free from dust as possible. Meadow hay is best as it will include grasses, clover,

dandelions and other beneficial wild plants. Buy it a bale at a time if you are keeping a number of rabbits. It must be stored in a dry place. You will need to replenish it each day. In the warmer months less will be needed than in the winter.

4. **Straw**. There are various types but generally it is not the ideal covering. It has little nutritional value, does not absorb urine very well, and it can be dangerous if sharp pieces were to catch the rabbit's eye.

5. **Woodshavings**. Better than straw as a top covering over sawdust in the living area - or as the sole covering. It is clean and easy to clear away. You can purchase pine bedding by Living World.

This **Nilotron@** aerosol automatic metered dispenser offers time released odor control. This is needed in every hutch. ➡

Living World Alfalfa is the ideal hay for rabbits.

The bottom of this type of Hagen cage should be half-filled with alfalfa as bedding and snacks for the rabbit. ◀

Pine Bedding by Living World is a very absorbent and inexpensive bedding.

Art. # 61230   Art. # 61231

Corn cobs by Living World are very absorbent and can be used to line the cage tray.

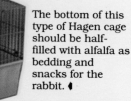

Pet shops sell rabbit pellets. ◄

◄ *Hagen Honey and Vegetable Sticks are a very good treat food.*

Feeding

Rabbits (and guinea pigs) are herbivorous, meaning they subsist on a plant and vegetable diet. Rather than eat one big meal they prefer to nibble away steadily over the day. This allows the strong cellulose walls of the plants and vegetables to be broken down so they are more readily absorbed into the body. In order to gain maximum benefit from their food, rabbits pass this twice through the digestive system.

Whilst cattle regurgitate their food (chewing the cud), rabbits pass special food pellets from their body and eat these. The process is known as refection or coprophagy. Often people will think the rabbit is eating its own fecal matter, but it is not. The two types of pellets are totally different, even though they both are passed from the anus.

Feeding Utensils

Any small dish will be quite adequate for use as a feeding dish. The best are those made from earthenware (crock), as they are long lasting and easy to clean. Additionally, they are heavy, a decided bonus in many instances as rabbits often develop the habit of picking up their feeding dish and throwing it about the hutch. Aluminum is another hygienic material - but it is light, as are plastic dishes. The latter will also be chewed by the rabbit so I wouldn't recommend them. Vegetables and fruits can simply be placed on the floor of the hutch, but they will then be coated in sawdust, so it is best to place them in a suitably deep dish - the same is true of oats, bran and mashes. Water can be fed in an open container, but this will soon be full of dust and sawdust, or tipped over by your pet, so it is best to use a rabbit water bottle obtained from your pet shop. These are made of glass or plastic and are filled with water before being inverted.

◄ A vitamin supplement can be added to your pet's diet. Hagen makes one especially for rabbits and other small animals.

From the cap of the bottle extends a short metal tube, which is fitted with a ball bearing in the end. As the rabbit licks this, it pushes it up and water flows out onto the tongue. Your pet will quickly learn how to use this. The water stays fresher and unspoiled by dirt. It must be changed daily and washed carefully once a week to remove any green algae which forms on its inner surfaces. It is usually supported from the hutch mesh by a wire, but it is better if you add an extra wire support further up the bottle so it is really secure.

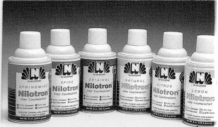

◆ *Nilotron@* is Nilodor's new environmentally improved aerosol odor neutralizer.

Hagen has a small animal mineral stone perfect for rabbits. ◆

Art. # H-10

◆ *Hagen Colds and Respiratory Aid* is excellent for treating sniffles and colds.

Suitable Foods

The first advice in feeding any animal is always that the food be as fresh as possible. With rabbits, you should also wash plant and vegetable matter just to be sure any dirt or crop chemicals are removed - these might be toxic to your pet. Chop all fruits into a size that is easy for the rabbit to cope with. The range of potential foods is vast so should provide no problem. Make it as interesting as possible. In this way, it will also be a balanced diet that ensures no important ingredients are missing. The diet will be composed of three basic parts:

1. **Plants and Vegetables**. These will include carrots, swedes, potatoes, turnips, lettuce, cauliflower, sprouts, peas, beans, apples, pears, tomatoes, grapes, strawberries and really any items that you would eat. To these you can add grass, hay, and many flowering plants (such as marigold, rose, aster, daisy and sunflower). Never feed plants that grow from bulbs and any plant you know to be poisonous. The latter assumes some knowledge of plants.

Fortunately, if you feed a wide variety of wild plants, such as dandelion, clover, parsley, yarrow, shepherd's purse or chickweed, any potentially toxic plants gathered with them will either be rejected by the rabbit or will be counteracted by the beneficial plants. Do not

Hagen Rabbit Treats are appreciated by rabbits. But most important is that good treats provide dietary supplements necessary for a healthy rabbit. ▶

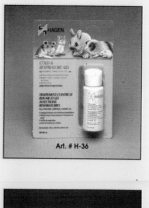

Art. # H-1163   Art. # H-1164

19

➤ Feed your rabbit pellets made especially for them. Add a carrot for variety. Only feed them fruits and vegetables that YOU would eat.

This is a harmless plant and, under normal circumstances, it may be fed to your pet rabbit. You must be sure, though, that it is free of pesticides. ➤

➤ Your pet store should have a Hagen Water Bottle, which releases water to the rabbit on demand when the rabbit licks the tip of the bottle.

Art. # H-69

Wild rabbits seem to know poisonous plants from safe ones. Don't take a chance. Do NOT offer your pet rabbit wild plants and flowers. ➤

gather wild plants from hedgerows that may have been subjected to automobile fumes or fouling by dogs. Avoid hedges next to fields that have been sprayed with toxic pesticides.

2. **Cereal Crops**. Rabbits enjoy oats, bran, maize, barley and most other cereal crops. These are fed dry or as part of a mixed moist mash. Bread is enjoyed (wholemeal is best) either fresh, hard or toasted. The latter is beneficial for rabbits' teeth as it provides something to gnaw on. Likewise, hard cookies will be enjoyed, but avoid too many sweet items as they are no better for your pet than they are for you!

3. **Other Items**. Rabbits are very cosmopolitan in

▼Your pet shop has plenty of rabbit feeds. Use only feeds specially formulated for rabbits. Add some fruit and carrots to make the meal more appetizing and nutritious.

their likes so by all means try them on a variety of items that you would eat. They like crusty pastry, cheese, milk, cakes and the like. They do not eat meat of course.

You will find that rabbits, whilst eating basically the same foods, will differ in their preferences. Some will eat grapes, others will not. Some will ignore tomatoes; others may partake small amounts of it. All will enjoy cereal crops and items such as carrots (including the tops) and foods which are normally found in the rabbit's wild environment.

4. **Mashes**. To prepare a mash, simply mix a whole collection of foods together and mash them into small pieces. To this add just enough warm water to make it moist. Mix again and feed. The basis of the mash can be bran, oats and other cereals to which you add crumpled bread, cheese, chopped vegetables and fruits and so on. This makes an interesting change from the regular diet. Mashes will quickly sour, especially in warm weather, and if milk has been added. Feed them in the late afternoon and discard any uneaten the following morning.

5. **Pellets**. Proprietary rabbit pellets contain all of the needed nutrients required by a rabbit. Commercial breeding establishments and laboratories feed their stock almost exclusively on these. They are easy to feed, store well and ensure a balanced diet. I think they are also boring if you feed your pet on them exclusively, so provide them in small quantities. This way, the rabbit enjoys them without having to subsist on them. Mixed bags of rabbit food from your pet shop will usually include pellets. Do remember that when feeding dry foods to your pet, its water intake will rise, so always check that the water bottle is operating correctly. In the winter, the nipple of the bottle sometimes freezes, even when the water hasn't, so check matters daily.

This little dwarf albino white has finished its pellets and has ignored the fruit. This is due to its not knowing that the fruit is good to eat. Many pet shop rabbits are fed only pellets, and they don't know about other fresh foods. Simply cut the apple or carrot into small pieces and add it to the pellets. ▶

Rabbits all eat the same. Feed fresh vegetables, like carrots, plus the usual pet store brand of rabbit food and your rabbit will live out its life in a normal and healthy manner. ◄

A well-fed Lop: A good—or poor—diet will be reflected in your rabbit's overall appearance. ◄

The amount of food that your rabbit consumes will be determined by his age, size, and level of activity.

Offering your dwarf rabbit (or any rabbit for that matter) fresh flowers is NOT advisable. Most such flowers are chemically treated with a pesticide and fertilizer.

Your pet will enjoy the chance to explore your garden. Just make sure that it has no access to poisonous plants.

When to Feed

Ideally, rabbits need two feeds per day: one in the morning and one in the late afternoon. Mashes are best given in the afternoon when the sun has lost much of its power. Fresh foods are best in the morning so any uneaten can be removed in the afternoon. Dry foods (pellets, oats, bran, hard bread, etc.) can be left to be eaten more or less ad lib - unless your pet becomes overweight. You will soon get to know if you are under or overfeeding and can adjust the amounts accordingly. Always remember, fresh foods and variety will help keep bunny happy and healthy.

It should be mentioned that if you have decided to keep a guinea pig as a companion to a rabbit, it cannot synthesize its own vitamin C, as can a rabbit. This vitamin must be supplied via the diet, or the guinea pig will become ill. If it has fresh greenfoods each day, then things will be fine, as these contain this important vitamin. You can also supply it via supplements, but it is best obtained in food.

Breeding

The breeding of rabbits is a fascinating pastime, but it is not without quite a number of problems. It should not be undertaken lightly. Rabbits are proverbial for their breeding ability, and the result of this is that there is no shortage of them. This means that casual breeders can end up with a lot of stock they cannot get rid of. In the end they often give them away in order to reduce the cost of keeping them. A litter of 6-10 babies grows up quickly. You must have sufficient extra space to accommodate them, and the extra food to feed them.

In general, it is probably best not to breed your pet rabbits unless they are of a definite breed and are good examples of it. In other words it is really only a worthwhile pursuit if you are interested in developing a stud of quality rabbits which will have exhibition and breeding potential. Even then you will find much of that produced falls short and is only suited to sale as pet stock. Rabbit breeding for show purposes is no money maker, so if you do decide to undertake this, you must not expect to come out financially to the good. At best it might defray a few costs.

◄Rabbits can be bred in the winter. As shown, the temperature of -22°C. (=about 8°F.) in the outside hutch does not disturb the babies, which are insulated in their bedding at 16°C. (=60°F.). The lower illustration shows indoor breeding quarters where the temperature rarely gets below freezing (0°C. = 32°F.)

Breeding Facts

It is possible for a female rabbit to have, in theory, 5-6 litters per year. However, this would place an enormous strain on her physical well being. This so, 2-3 would be a suggested maximum if the object was to rear strong

The *English Spot* rabbit is a very attractive pet rabbit. ▶

An experience person, especially a veterinarian, can usually tell by feel if a rabbit is pregnant. ☞

Note the tattoo in this rabbit's ear. It indicates that the rabbit is registered with a national organization. ☞

The markings on this Polish white are called *Himalayan.* ☞

healthy youngsters. Spring and summer are the best times to breed rabbits, as this corresponds with longer daylight hours and a plentiful supply of greenfoods.

Rabbits reach breeding age when they are from 5-8 months old, depending on the breed. The small- to medium-sized breeds mature faster than the larger ones. An average litter will range from 5-10 babies, and these are born naked and quite helpless after a gestation period of 30-33 days. They will feed on their mother's milk for about three weeks, at which time they will begin to nibble on oats, greens and similar foods. They are normally weaned and fully independent of the mother by the time they are 5-8 weeks of age, the latter being the best age.

Their fur commences growing almost as soon as they are born, and by about the fourth day it is clearly visible. Their eyes begin to open when they are 7-10 days old.

Breeding Procedure

You can sex your rabbits by inspecting their anal region. The rabbit will need to be mature before you can tell with certainty which sex it is. In the case of the female, her anal opening is quite close to her vulva, which is narrow and long when compared to the penial opening of the male. The male will also have its testes apparent in its scrotal sac.

The doe (female) is always taken to the buck when a mating is to be attempted. He will chase the female around the hutch for a while, but if the doe is ready for mating, she will eventually stay still when a mating will be effected. After a short rest, further matings will take place. If the doe refuses to mate and fights the buck, she should be removed and tried again a few days later. Some does are slower ovulaters and take longer to be induced into shedding eggs for fertilization - in other words to be prepared to accept a male.

It is unwise to leave the female overnight in a hutch with the male. He may pester her to the degree that she becomes very stressed, and this is never a desired condition. It is sometimes possible to tell if a doe is 'in kindle' by carefully feeling her abdomen about 12-14 days after the mating, when the growing fetuses may be felt. Alternatively, place the doe with the buck about a week after a mating. If she totally rejects him, this usually indicates she is pregnant. It will become very apparent that a doe is carrying offspring during the last 7-10 days before she gives birth, that is, about three weeks after she was mated.

Once the doe has been mated, she must be handled with great care, progressively more so as the pregnancy advances. After about a week, she will start to prepare a nest lining by biting fur from her abdomen and by gathering bedding material into a corner of her sleeping compartment. You could supply her with a nest box so that she is more snug and so that the babies are more easily retained in the warmth of it. Once the doe is mated, she must be separated from the buck from that time onward, until the youngsters are weaned. Some bucks can safely be left with youngsters, but others might attack them; so it is best not to take chances until you really know your stock.

Birth and Rearing

In most instances, a doe will have her litter with no trouble at all. Sometimes a maiden doe having her first litter may become frightened and abandon or even eat the babies - the more so if she has

The health of your rabbit depends upon the cleanliness of its hutch. **Nilodor** makes a cleaner that also deodorizes. It is ideal for rabbits...and safe too. ☚

In preparation for winter breeding, boxes are filled loosely with hay. The rabbits make a nest deep within the hay and the walls of the boxes ensure that the babies are free of drafts. ☚

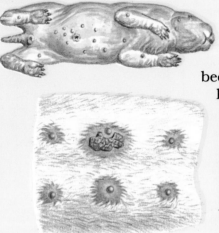

◀ A *Staphylococcus* infection on the skin of a newborn rabbit.

A *Staph* infection under the skin. ▲

A *Staph* infection on the paws. Staph infections are easily treated with antibiotics. Consult your local veterinarian. ▲

A mixed breed rabbit with a color pattern that resembles that of the English Spot. ▼

been disturbed by something. Even your looking into the nest daily could create such a situation, so it is always best to leave the doe alone when a birth is imminent. This should prevail for about a week. Thereafter you can check on the babies to see if they are alright, but handle the doe first so your hands carry her scent before you touch the babies.

You can check on the babies at any time if you have arranged things so that you can see in the nest whilst the mother has been tempted away with some tasty morsels to eat. If a doe proves to be a bad mother over two or more litters, then it is best to cease breeding from her, as this trait is hereditary. When the youngsters are fully weaned, they can be left with their mother if she is not to be bred from straight away, or they can be transferred to a large stock cage and run until they are sold. Whilst the babies should be given plenty of good food so they put on good weight, do be careful that they do not gorge on greenfoods suddenly as the latter become more available. This will only result in upset stomachs. This of course applies to the adults. Many novice owners tend to overfeed wild plants as these become available in the spring. Introduce greenfoods gradually - good advice in respect of any foods which your rabbits are not familiar with.

Fostering

If you keep a number of rabbits for breeding, should one mother die, or prove to be a bad mother, you can always foster babies to another doe with babies of about the same age. To make the transfer, wipe your hands over the foster mother or even rub your hands in some of her soiled bedding. The orphans are then well rubbed before being placed amongst the foster mother's litter. Of course, you should not overload her with youngsters if she already has a large litter.

This is a *New Zealand* red rabbit. It is primarily bred for its meat.

False (Phantom) Pregnancy

It may happen that a female is placed into a hutch that previously contained a buck. She

An *English Lop* or *Ram* rabbit. In a good specimen of the breed, ear length (from tip to tip) will be at least 21".

The *Silver* rabbit is bred for both food and fur. It is found in black, brown and fawn. This is a male.

may also pick up the scent of a nearby buck, or may even be induced to ovulate by does in the same hutch. In any of these circumstances, she may commence a false pregnancy. She is convinced she is having babies and goes through all the phases as she would if she had been mated. She might even convince you she was pregnant unless you knew this was not possible! No babies will result, and she can be brought out of this state by being placed with a buck.

This is a female *Silver*.

A *Rhinelander* rabbit. ➤

Which Breed?

Rabbits, in general terms, can be divided between those regarded as fancy breeds and those which are termed fur breeds. The latter include breeds also bred for meat. Fur breeds may be normal coated, rex haired, or rough coated. The fancy breeds are the most popular pet and exhibition rabbits but certain of the others are also very well supported in shows - especially the rex varieties with their plush, velvet-like fur.

In terms of size, which is usually an important consideration for a pet, you can choose between dwarf and small breeds, average-sized breeds, and finally the large heavy breeds. The other feature that will certainly be high on your priorities is that of color and pattern. The range is almost unlimited, whether this be in recognizable breeds or simply in mixed-breed rabbits. With so many combinations to choose from, it will be well worthwhile having a good look around before making your choice. The breeds discussed in this chapter are but a sampling of the 40-plus breeds you can choose from. They are graded by size rather than by official category.

A *Dwarf Lop* rabbit. ➤

Dwarf rabbits are best for house pets. They are barely larger than a guinea pig. ➤

A *Marburg Squirrel* rabbit. This breed is found in Eastern Europe. ➤

Dwarf Breeds

The smallest of the rabbits is the Netherland Dwarf, which should weigh about 2 lbs. It has short ears (ideally 2 in. long), large round eyes and a domed, broad skull. It is a real cute little bunny, but you should be sure its teeth are well aligned. In its developmental years, these were a source of problems. The range of colors is vast and is divided into five groups. These are comprised of just about every color and combination possible in rabbits. It is an economical rabbit to keep and has a tremendous specialty following.

The Polish is another dwarf, being only slightly heavier than the Netherland. It was originally a pure albino breed but these days is seen in as many colors as is its Dutch counterpart. Like all small rabbits it will have only small litters, that is, few babies. The British Polish is better known in the USA as the Britannia Petite.

If you like the long-eared lop breed but not its size, then the dwarf lop should please you. It is 4 $^1/_2$ lbs. in weight and is a pretty little breed seen in a useful range of colors and patterns. There is now a cashmere lop with longer fur, but it should not be woolly as its name might suggest, just long and silky. The dwarf lops are a better proposition as pets than their larger relatives, but watch out for any protruding nails or netting that could cut into their pendant ears. These breeds are also more prone to ear problems, so do inspect them on a regular basis.

Medium-Sized Breeds

In this size group are to be found most of the breeds usually selected as pets. Possibly the most widely known rabbit is the Dutch. Its body color is divided between white at the front and a color on the rear part of its body. There is a white wedge-shaped blaze on the face, and the paws of the rear feet are also white. It is very difficult to breed well-marked exhibition stock. Colors are black, blue, chocolate, yellow, steel gray, brown gray, pale gray, and tortoiseshell. The tricolored Dutch is very pretty but now very rare. Other colors, such as cinnamon, are seen

A dwarf rabbit with a nice coat and fawn color. ➤

The chinchilla coloration is very popular in rabbits. ➤

A lovely black Satin. This is a pet breed. ➤

29

The hairs of the Angora rabbit can be pulled out to get them to maximum length. This *plucking* is not comfortable for most rabbits, but it can be tolerated.

After plucking the Angora should look like this.

You can also cut the hair of the Angora rabbit, but then you do not get the best length of fur fibers.

but not officially accepted at this time. The Dutch weighs about 4 1/2 lbs.

Another popular breed is the English. This is white with a colored (there are five recognized) unbroken herringbone stripe down its back. It has colored ears and eye rings and a colored smut which should be butterfly shaped. The body carries variably sized spots. As with the Dutch, this is a very difficult rabbit to produce to good exhibition standards because the markings often fall short of those desired. It weighs about 7 lbs. and makes a delightful pet.

If dark colors appeal to you, then you might like the Tan. This has the body, face and ears in solid black with an eye ring, inner ear, throat and underparts in tan. The contrast is extremely attractive. There are now blue, chocolate and lilac varieties, in each case the color replacing the black, not the tan. The weight is around 4 1/2 lbs. Staying with dark colors, the Silver Fox is a beautiful breed. It is black with silver tipped hairs on its body and with white under its jaws. There are also blue, chocolate, and lilac foxes. Weight is about 6 lbs. A very well-known pattern in rabbits (and in other small pets such as mice, cats, rats) is seen on the Himalayan breed. This may be a smallish breed at about 5 lbs., or a heavy variety reaching 11 lbs. The body is white, whilst the ears, smut, paws and tail are black. It is always a favorite when seen. It should not be confused with the Californian, which has the same markings and was bred by

LEFT: *ENCYCLOPEDIA OF PET RABBITS* by D. Robinson is a 320-page book with almost 300 illustrations. **CENTER:** *LOP RABBITS AS PETS* by Sandy Crook is the best book on lops. **RIGHT:** *STARTING RIGHT WITH RABBITS* by Mervin F. Roberts is a standard book on rabbit keeping. ALL OF THESE BOOKS ARE AVAILABLE FROM YOUR LOCAL PET SUPPLIER.

crossings to it with other breeds. The alternate colors are blue, chocolate or lilac. This pattern is heat sensitive, meaning that it fades the warmer the climate, a point worth noting if you live in such a zone.

Moving from coat color to fur type, two breeds are significant. The Satin has a beautiful silk fur with a really outstanding sheen to it. It weighs about 7 lbs. The fur is not as dense as normal fur and the colors tend to be darker than their equivalents in normal fur. The breed is seen in a very extensive range of colors.

The Rex breed always results in great interest because it is so impressive. The short fur is dense and really like velvet to the touch. It is created by the guard hairs growing only the same length as the woolly undercoat. The mutation is inherited independently of color so most colors and patterns are seen in the breed. It has been developed to a very high standard of perfection. The full coat does not appear until after the rabbit's first molt at maturity. Weight is about 7 lbs. You can also have a Satin Rex and an Opossum Rex, the latter with long, stiff hairs tipped in silver.

Large Breeds

The large fur breeds are not really the ideal rabbits to have as pets. They have the same fine temperaments as all rabbits but obviously they will cost more to care for and require more space. If these aspects are not a problem, then the Chinchilla is a nice breed. It varies in weight depending on the country and may range from 6 lbs. to maybe 15 lbs. Its fur is famous for being used to make gloves, being

This is a British-bred *Polish* rabbit with the markings of a Himalayan.

A *Mini-Rex* rabbit.

◆ **LEFT:** *RABBITS AS A HOBBY* is a great new book. The profits go to save the planet! **CENTER:** *A STEP-BY-STEP BOOK ABOUT RABBITS* by Anmarie Barrie. A good book for beginners. **RIGHT:** *YOUR FIRST RABBIT* is a small book which should accompany every rabbit sold to a novice. YOUR PET SHOP HAS EVERY ONE OF THESE BOOKS.

A female *English Spot.* ◆

extremely soft and sleek. The color is a mixture of steel blue, black and white. The New Zealand white is a large and popular breed of 9-12 lbs., the doe being heavier than the buck. It is a true albino with red eyes and no color pigment at all on its white body. It was developed in the USA. There is also a New Zealand black and a red, whilst a blue has been developed in Great Britain.

Two very old breeds are the Flemish Giant and the Beveren. The former is found under different names all over the world. It may reach 20 lbs. in weight, but most are rather lighter. Colors are variable but are usually agouti with white underparts, rather like wild rabbits. The Beveren is a blue-furred breed that weighs 8 lbs. or more. It is now seen in other colors but, sadly, is one of a number of old breeds that are declining in popularity.

Other large breeds are the Belgian Hare (not a true hare), the Checkered Giant, the Californian and the Blanc de Hotot (a pure white breed with a black eye ring). Do visit a large rabbit show before making your selection, because it costs just as much money to keep and feed a nice purebred as it does a rabbit of mixed ancestry. Purebreds are surprisingly inexpensive if you want only a pet - even good show-standard examples are cheap when compared to puppies or kittens.

◆Rabbits with long fur require constant grooming if they are to look their best. Your local pet shop has grooming tools.

◆ This broken black *American Fuzzy Lop* is being brushed preparatory for an exhibition.